D1477873

CASTLES
OF THE WORLD

CASTLES
OF THE WORLD

PHYLLIS G. JESTICE

amber
BOOKS

First published in 2021

Copyright © 2021 Amber Books Ltd

Published by
Amber Books Ltd
United House
North Road
London
N7 9DP
United Kingdom
www.amberbooks.co.uk
Instagram: amberbooksltd
Facebook: amberbooks
Twitter: @amberbooks
Pinterest: amberbooksltd

Project Editor: Michael Spilling
Designers: Zoe Mellors
Picture Research: Justin Willsdon

ISBN: 978-1-83886-098-1
Printed in China

Contents

Introduction

Castles – fortified outposts designed to protect or dominate a territory – have been constructed at least since the Bronze Age. Unlike fortified towns, castles were not primarily intended to accommodate populations, but rather through most of history have housed a small garrison of military professionals, as well as the controlling noble's family. Castles vary widely in design, depending on the availability of building materials and technological sophistication, including

structures built of rammed earth, wood, stone, brick and steel-reinforced concrete. But in their original purpose, they express a basic truth: it was more economical to build a stronghold that could be held by a few men than it was to maintain a large body of soldiers.

Castles were natural objects of prestige, since the noble who controlled a castle could dominate the surrounding countryside. Inevitably, they became such status symbols that nobles constructed castles as their family homes, even when the need for defence had long passed. They evoke an imagined age of noble warriors and aspirations for which many people still yearn today.

ABOVE:
Amra Castle, Jordan
Frescoes decorate the walls of this 8th-century Umayyad stronghold.
OPPOSITE:
Theodosian Walls, Istanbul
First constructed in the 5th century CE, the Theodosian Walls were not breached for a thousand years.

Ancient Times to 700 CE

While humans built castles from very early in our history, few of these ancient fortifications still survive in anything like the form they were first constructed. The reason is simple: our ancestors had a good eye for defensible locations, so most often the same site was used again and again through history. Later generations added fortifications and made alterations to suit the needs of their own age.

Archaeologists have puzzled out the early history of some of these ancient fortifications, such as the Tower of David in Jerusalem, which has been rebuilt a dozen times in the two millennia of its existence. But the best hope to see an ancient fortification as it might have appeared to contemporaries is to visit a site that is now a backwater; a place that, after a brief moment of significance, was for the most part forgotten. These sites, whether Iron Age fortresses in the British Isles or the great Mycenaean citadels from the era of the Trojan War, can still inspire us with awe at the engineering acumen of our ancestors.

OPPOSITE:
Rayen Citadel, Iran
Rayen Citadel is at least a thousand years old, and its foundations may date from before the Islamic conquests of the 7th century CE. As the citadel of a major trade centre, this large (22,000 sq m; 236,806 sq ft) adobe castle gave stability to the region as well as housing several thousand families.

ALL PHOTOGRAPHS:

David's Citadel, Jerusalem, Israel

Also known as the Citadel of Jerusalem, the Tower of David's history goes back at least 2,000 years, when the Hasmonean Dynasty expanded Jerusalem and erected a tower near the Jaffa Gate. Repeatedly rebuilt over the centuries, the Tower owes its current shape to Mamluk rebuilding c. 1310; the Ottomans expanded it in the 16th century.

Arg-E Bam, Iran

Arg-E Bam is the largest adobe building in the world. The citadel covers an 18-hectare (44-acre) site surrounded by a massive wall over 1.6km (1 mile) long. The Achaemenid Persians (5th century bce) built the earliest fortress on the site; its key location on the Silk Road assured its prosperity for millennia. Arg-E Bam was almost completely destroyed by an earthquake in 2003. The photograph shows the site before the earthquake.

ALL PHOTOGRAPHS:

Gongsanseong Castle, South Korea

Gongsanseong Castle was constructed in c. 475 CE, when the Baekje Kingdom of southwestern Korea moved its capital to Gongju. One of the many hill castles that attest to Korea's war-torn past, Gongsanseong was restored in 1993 and is now a UNESCO World Heritage site.

ABOVE:
Samuil's Fortress, Ohrid, Macedonia
Dominating the city of Ohrid, this citadel was the work
of the Bulgar Tsar Samuil at the end of the 10th century
CE, although excavations suggest that the first fortress
on the site dates to the time of Philip II of Macedon in
the 4th century BCE. With walls standing 15.8m (52ft)
high (restored in 2003), the fortress is an impressive
monument to one of the Balkans' strongest rulers.

OPPOSITE:
Citadel, Berat, Albania
With a sheer drop to the Osum River to the north,
Berat Citadel's highly defensible location explains why
a fortress has stood here for about 2500 years. Destroyed
by the Romans in 200 BCE, the citadel was rebuilt in the
6th and 13th centuries, expanding to defend an area
large enough for much of the town's population to
live inside.

Durrës Castle, Albania
The old city of Durrës was first fortified by the Eastern Roman Emperor Anastasius in the late 5th century CE, although most of the current structure was built after the castle was largely destroyed in an earthquake in 1273.

In April 1939, a small group of Albanians held off the Italian invasion of their country at Durrës, but the walls could not withstand Italian tanks.

Skopje Fortress, Macedonia

Commonly known as *Kale* (from the Turkish word for 'fortress'), Skopje's castle was first constructed in the 6th century CE, probably at the order of the Roman Emperor Justinian. The engineers used stone from the Roman town, which had been destroyed in an earthquake.

Al-Ukhaidir Fortress, Karbala, Iraq

In its current form, Al-Ukhaidir dates to 775 CE, when an Abbasid prince built it as a retirement residence, but its roots date to the Sassanian Persians (3rd–7th centuries CE). Standing in the desert, Al-Ukhaidir is a good example of Abbasid defensive architecture.

Early Medieval Period: 700–1200

Other parts of the world, such as China and the Middle East, had long built stone fortresses, but medieval Europe only followed suit starting in the 10th century. Europeans gradually replaced simple wooden forts and motte-and-bailey fortresses (artificial mounds with a stockade at the summit) with more durable structures made from stone. Most often, castles began as a simple keep or bailey – a single strongly-built stone dwelling that could be secured by removing the staircase that led up to the entrance. Gradually, owners improved on these small forts by constructing curtain walls with defensive towers – which also allowed them to accommodate many more defenders. The entryways to these expanded castles were protected by strong gatehouses, often with a heavy portcullis that could be lowered to provide an additional barrier. The strongest castles were on an island or surrounded by a moat, filled with either water or sharpened stakes.

OPPOSITE:
Tourbillon Castle, Switzerland
Built in the late 13th century by the powerful prince-bishop of Sion, Tourbillon Castle for much of its history was hated and attacked as a symbol of episcopal power. Much of the castle was rebuilt after rebels devastated it early in the 15th century, and it was mostly destroyed in 1788, only to be restored in the 20th century.

Ribat Castle, Monastir, Tunisia
One of North Africa's best-preserved and oldest castles, Ribat was constructed in 796 CE by the Abbasid governor of the region. Situated on the Mediterranean Sea, for centuries the fortress protected Monastir from pirate attacks, and also served as a base for local warlords.

Qasr Kharana, Jordan
An early example of an Islamic fortress, Qasr Kharana was built in the early 8th century. The square building consists of 60 rooms across two storeys around a central courtyard. Its purpose is mysterious, since it was never very defensible, did not lie on a popular trade route, and lacked a good water source.

ABOVE:
Hochosterwitz Castle, Austria

This limestone rock has been inhabited since the Bronze Age. Since the 12th century, it has been home to Austria's most impressive castle, parts of which date from the 16th century. The 14 gates protecting the steep path shows why it was never successfully assaulted.

RIGHT:
Blagaj Fort, Bosnia & Herzegovina

The earliest parts of today's castle date to the 4th and 6th centuries CE. There was a medieval expansion of the whole site, and reinforcement of the walls in the late 14th and early 15th centuries to provide better protection against gunpowder weapons.

Rabati Castle, Akhaltsikhe, Georgia

Established in the 9th century, Rabati Castle in its current form dates to the 13th century, but was substantially rebuilt by the Ottomans in the 17th and 18th centuries. Despite its imposing construction, Rabati Castle was successfully stormed in the Battle of Akhaltsikhe (1828), after which the region passed from Ottoman control into Russian hands.

Kantara Castle, Cyprus
Kantara is one of three castles that the Byzantines constructed along the Kyrenian Mountains, probably in the late 11th century. In the 13th century, it withstood a year-long siege in the wars for control of the Kingdom of Jerusalem; otherwise it served as a prison and a watchtower against pirates.

RIGHT:

Pembroke Castle, Wales
In 1093, Norman invaders built the first castle on the promontory at Pembroke, the water providing a natural defence on three sides. When William Marshal was given the site in 1189, he replaced the motte-and-bailey fortification with the stone keep seen today.

LEFT:

Rudkhan Castle, Iran
Approached by means of a
1,000-step climb, Rudkhan
is a brick castle perched
on two mountain peaks
linked with ramparts and
42 towers. The Sassanian
Persians first fortified it in
the 6th or 7th century, but
the castle was rebuilt in
the Seljuk period (11–12th
centuries).

OPPOSITE:

Citadel of Aleppo, Syria
Fortified at least since the
3rd century BCE, Citadel
Hill in Aleppo is an
enormous military and
administrative centre.
In around 1200 CE,
following Saladin's defeat
of the Crusaders, his son
expanded the castle to its
current state, most notably
smoothing the slope of
the hill and lining it with
stone to form a glacis.

OPPOSITE:

Castle of Leiria, Portugal

When Afonso Henriques, first king of Portugal, took Leiria in 1142, he developed the castle to defend the region from Moorish reconquest. In its first decades, Leiria withstood two Muslim sieges, but declined in importance after the Christian conquest of Lisbon. In the 14th century it was remodelled as a royal residence.

ABOVE:

Loarre Castle, Huesca, Spain

One of Spain's oldest castles, Loarre was erected in stages between c. 1020 and the early 12th century to support the early steps of the Christian reconquest of the Iberian Peninsula. Constructed on a rocky outcrop that prevented a single unified plan, it consists of a number of buildings surrounded by curtain walls.

ALL PHOTOGRAPHS:
Leeds Castle, Kent, England

Site of a stronghold since 1086, Leeds Castle was rebuilt in stone in 1119. It avoided destruction in the English Civil War (1642–1651) because the owner of the time supported Parliament; parliamentary forces used the castle as an arsenal and a prison during the conflict.

Although today the castle may appear to be a Tudor stronghold from the 16th century, in fact most of its fabric dates from the early 1800s: following the sale of extensive estates in Virginia, USA, the owners remodelled Leeds to fit their early romantic notions of what a castle should look like.

ALL PHOTOGRAPHS:
Beaufort Castle, Luxembourg
Beaufort had its start in the early 11th century as a small square stone building protected by a moat. A keep was added in the first half of the 12th century, with further additions in the 1340s. In the 16th century the owner stayed in touch with the times by adding a Renaissance wing.

Beaufort fell derelict and was abandoned at the time of the French Revolution (1789–99); for a time the site was even used as a quarry. Fortunately, in 1893 the castle's owner decided on a programme of renovation, opening the castle to the public in 1928.

Windsor Castle, England
Now the longest-occupied palace in Europe, the first castle at Windsor was constructed in the late 11th century after the Norman invasion.

Later, following the Restoration of the monarchy in 1660, Charles II rebuilt the castle with Baroque state apartments that survive today. The Round Tower *(right)* is based on an original 12th-century building, but was extensively remodelled in the 19th century.

Still a royal residence for Queen Elizabeth II, today parts of Windsor are open to the public. The Queen holds state banquets there and the wedding of Prince Harry to Meghan Markle took place in St George's Chapel at Windsor in 2018.

Vianden Castle, Luxembourg

One of the largest fortified castles west of the River Rhine, Vianden was in good shape until 1820, when a purchaser provoked such outcry by beginning demolition that the king bought the site back.

The castle was built on the site of a Roman *castellum* (a small fort). It began as a keep with residential apartments c. 1100, but the count of Vianden added a new two-storey palace in the early 13th century, displaying plainly the family's pretensions to power in the region.

43

Peyrepertuse, France

Located high in the French Pyrenees, Peyrepertuse became a stronghold of the Christian Cathar sect in the early 13th century. Unlike other Cathar castles in the region, it was not besieged during the Albigensian Crusade (1209–29), but surrendered to the French crusaders. Having lost its strategic importance on the Franco–Spanish border, the castle was decommissioned in 1659.

Chillon Castle, Switzerland

Chillon, situated on a small island on Lake Geneva, guards the strategic road from Burgundy to the Great St Bernard Pass. The castle's first mention in a written source dates from 1005, and it owes most if its current appearance to the count of Savoy's rebuilding in 1248. Since it was strongly built, Chillon was frequently used as a prison from the 14th through the 17th centuries. Starting in 1880 and continuing into the early 20th century, Chillon was restored to its medieval glory.

ALL PHOTOGRAPHS:
Aigle Castle, Switzerland
Most of Aigle's current fabric dates to the second half of the 13th century, when a fortified keep and curtain wall were constructed on the site. Badly damaged in the Burgundian Wars of 1474–77, the castle was rebuilt in 1488 and became the headquarters of the provincial governor.

After the French Revolution, Aigle Castle lost its administrative significance; from 1804 to 1976 it served as the local jail. Today it is open to tourists and is home to a Vine and Wine Museum, thanks to its location in the midst of a major wine-producing region.

ALL PHOTOGRAPHS:
Burg Eltz, Germany
Perched above the Moselle River between Koblenz and Trier, Eltz Castle has been owned by the Eltz family ever since the 12th century. The keep dates to the 12th century, but Eltz above all owes its security to the Elzbach River, which surrounds it on three sides, and its position on a rock spur. Eltz was more impressive before it endured a two-year siege in the 1330s; after capitulating, the outer defences were demolished, leaving the castle as a simpler fortified residence. Branches of the family owned the castle in common, occupying more than one hundred residential rooms.

Castle Vaduz, Liechtenstein

A keep was constructed on the site of Vaduz in the 12th century and living quarters were added in 1287. Damaged in the Swabian War of 1499, the castle was subsequently rebuilt and the west side expanded in the 17th century. It is now the official residence of the prince of Liechtenstein.

Gutenberg Castle, Liechtenstein

The natural hill at Balzers has been inhabited since Neolithic times. Unsettled conditions in the German empire in the early 12th century led the local count to replace the church on the site with a fortified keep. Much of the castle still dates from the 12th century; Emperor Maximilian I renovated it in the early 16th century.

Bled Castle, Slovenia
Standing on a sheer cliff nearly 300m (1,000ft) above Lake Bled, for 800 years Bled Castle was the chief residence of the bishops of Brixen. The main tower dates to the 12th century, with early modern elements added.

OPPOSITE:
Spiš Castle, Slovakia
One of Europe's largest castles in area, Spiš was begun in the 12th century. A settlement formed in its shadow, which was then incorporated into the castle with an encircling wall. As further settlements were established, more expansive walls were built in the 14th and 15th centuries. Abandoned in the 18th century, the castle has been restored.

ALL PHOTOGRAPHS:

Asen's Fortress, Bulgaria
Standing in Bulgaria's
Rhodope Mountains,
this fortress has guarded
the state's western
frontier since the 11th
century. After Frederick I
Barbarossa's forces took
the castle when going
through Bulgaria on the
Third Crusade (1189–
92), Tsar Ivan Asen II
strengthened the defences
against further incursions.

The best-preserved part
of Asen's Fortress is the
Church of the Mother
of God (*below*), a fine
Byzantine-style building
that dates to the 12th
and 13th centuries. The
castle fell derelict after the
Ottoman conquest, but
local Christians continued
to use the fortress's chapel
as their parish church.

ALL PHOTOGRAPHS:
Hever Castle, Kent, England

Hever is deceptive: outside it appears to be a medieval fortress, but inside it is a gracious home. When the Boleyn family acquired Hever in 1462, they added a 'modern' house inside the existing walls, which, along with the bailey, date to 1270. Anne Boleyn, Henry VIII's second wife, grew up here. After serving as the Boleyn family home from 1462 to 1539, Henry VIII granted Hever to his fourth wife, Anne of Cleves, as part of the settlement following the annulment of their marriage.

In 1903 the American millionaire William Waldorf Astor purchased the castle, lavishly restoring it; his family used it as a residence until 1983.

ALL PHOTOGRAPHS:
**Stokesay Castle,
Shropshire, England**
Stokesay is one of the best-preserved manor houses in England, thanks especially to thoughtful restoration in the 19th century that didn't attempt to alter its appearance.

The 'castle' was built in the late 13th century by a major local wool merchant, who imitated the style of Edward I's Welsh castles.

Although called a castle, Stokesay was not constructed to withstand a serious assault. In 1645, a Parliamentary army besieged the castle, soon forcing the garrison to surrender. The castle was slighted (purposely damaged to make it unusable as a fortress), but remained habitable. Key features, including the hall with its 13th-century wood-beamed ceiling, survived intact.

LEFT:

Tourbillon Castle, Switzerland

Tourbillon Castle, on the hill to the left, dominates the town of Sion from one of the twin rocky outcrops that stand on the flank of the Alps. It can only be reached by a long, winding stairway. The other hill, to the right, is home to the Basilique de Valère, a Catholic basilica constructed in the 11th to 13th centuries.

ABOVE:

Loket Castle, Czech Republic

Known as 'The Impregnable Castle of Bohemia', Loket's history as a stone fortress goes back to the 12th century. Ottokar II added the curtain wall and a series of towers in the later 13th century. Hussite Christian reformers tried twice to take the castle in the 15th century, but both sieges ended in failure.

ALL PHOTOGRAPHS:

Orava Castle, Slovakia

Orava was fortified in 1267, following the Mongol invasion of Hungary. The castle was substantially remodelled in the 16th century. Legend tells that a noble made a pact with the devil: if the devil built Orava Castle in a single night, he could claim the nobleman's soul. But the task proved too difficult for Satan; the castle was not quite complete at dawn, so the nobleman's soul was saved – and he had a fine new castle.

Orava stands on a 112m (367ft) high rock spur above the Orava River. The upper castle, the citadel, is the oldest part of the complex.

Alcázar de Segovia, Castile and León, Spain

'Alcázar' is Arabic for a castle or palace, but the Segovia structure owes its shape to the Christian rulers of Castile. Alfonso VIII of Castile began converting the Almoravid fort to stone in c. 1200; John II (1406–54) added its most distinctive feature, the 'new tower', and Philip II decorated the castle with tall spires in the 16th century.

Turaida Castle, Latvia

The Catholic military order the Sword Brethren started construction of Turaida in 1214. When they merged with the Teutonic Order, the latter continued to develop the fortifications into the 15th century, building with the distinctive red brick of the Baltic. Left in ruins, Turaida Castle was reconstructed in the 1970s–1990s.

ALL PHOTOGRAPHS:

Malbork Castle, Poland

The Teutonic Knights began construction of Malbork (then known as Marienburg) in 1274 after suppressing a major Prussian revolt. It became headquarters of the order in 1309; frequent additions, creating three connected castles, were necessary to house an eventual 3,000 resident brethren. The castle reached its final state in 1406. In terms of area, Malbork is the largest castle in the world. Its strong fortifications allowed the Teutonic Order to survive after its great defeat at the Battle of Grunwald (1410), but the order was forced to cede their mighty headquarters to Poland with the second Treaty of Torun in 1466.

Kalmar Castle, Sweden
In the 12th century, a
tower was built to protect
Kalmar's harbour. Inside,
the castle was transformed
into a luxurious palace in
the 16th century.

OPPOSITE BOTTOM:
Örebro Castle, Sweden
Located on an island in
the Svartån River, the
earliest part of Örebro
Castle dates back to
the second half of the
13th century.

ABOVE:
Vyborg Castle, Russia
After the Third Swedish
Crusade against the
pagan Karelians tightened
Swedish control over
Finland, the new royal
governor ordered

construction of Vyborg
Castle in 1293 on an island
at the northeast corner
of the Gulf of Finland.
A small town originally
lay within the walls, but
changed location to gain
more space.

Castle Rushen, Isle of Man

The keep of Castle Rushen was probably constructed in the late 12th or early 13th century by the king of the Isles to guard the entrance to the Silverburn River. The curtain wall and towers were added in the 14th century. This is one of the best-preserved medieval castles in the British Isles.

Late Medieval Period: 1200–1500

Military architecture had to face a new challenge in the period after 1200: gunpowder weapons. Already the Mongols employed simple gunpowder grenades against enemy walls; a great breakthrough was learning how to harness the force of exploding gunpowder to hurl a projectile. Early cannon were unwieldy and often more dangerous to their owners than to the enemy, but they had potential, especially after new gunpowder preparation techniques increased potency. Straight walls were vulnerable to cannon balls, as were rectangular towers from which the corners could be knocked. Gradually, military castle design responded to the challenge, creating curved walls that were thicker and lower.

But non-military design also moved to new prominence. In more peaceful regions, nobles constructed palaces that included some elements of castle design, but were not in fact defensible in the face of a serious attack. The castle had become a symbol of prestige.

OPPOSITE:
Castello Aragonese, Island of Ischia, Italy
First fortified in 474 BCE, for millennia Castello Aragonese defended the Bay of Naples. The present castle and name come from the rebuilding of the castle by Alfonso V of Aragon in 1441. Castello Aragonese was badly damaged by British bombardment in 1809, but restored in the 20th century.

ALL PHOTOGRAPHS:

Alcázar of Seville, Spain

Constructed as a fortified residence for King Pedro the Cruel of Castile in the 14th century, the Alcázar of Seville is an outstanding example of the Iberian Peninsula's Mudéjar architecture, a Christian style that adopted many elements of Arabic art.

The most critical need for a castle under attack is a secure water supply. Lacking a river or groundwater source, the Alcázar's designers constructed a great rainwater cistern, named the 'Baths of Lady Maria di Padilla' (*see opposite*) in honour of King Pedro the Cruel's mistress.

ALL PHOTOGRAPHS:
La Alhambra, Granada, Spain
The opulent Alhambra was the chief residence of the Muslim emirs of Granada for the last century and a half before the Christian conquest of Granada in 1492. They created a great palace complex, which the new Christian monarchs, Isabella and Ferdinand, later renovated in the Renaissance style.

Built by order of the emir of Granada in the mid-13th century, the Alhambra was constructed on the remains of a 9th-century fort, itself built atop a Roman *castellum*.

Ananuri, Georgia

The oldest parts of Ananuri date to the 13th century; it saw many battles, which took place as recently as the 18th century. The complex now consists of two castles, linked together by a curtain wall; the upper castle is well preserved. Other buildings within the walls include two 17th-century churches.

OPPOSITE:

Eilean Donan Castle, Scotland
Standing on a small tidal island in the western Highlands, Eilean Donan was a stronghold of the Mackenzie clan, constructed in the 13th century. The Mackenzies supported the Jacobite rebellion of 1719, and a naval bombardment left the castle in ruins.

RIGHT:

Castle Stalker, Scotland
Castle Stalker is a four-storey keep on an islet in Loch Laich. Originally constructed in the early 14th century, it reached its present form in c. 1440. Castle Stalker is most famous in modern times for its use in the final scene of the film *Monty Python and the Holy Grail* (1975).

RIGHT:

Markovi Kuli, Macedonia

'Marko's Towers' is a fortress constructed in the early 14th century. It served as the palace for King Vukašin of Serbia and his son Prince Marko. Perched on a steep granite hill, the rampart of Markovi Kuli is still in good condition.

OPPOSITE:

Belogradchik Fortress, Bulgaria

A fortress has stood on the site of Belogradchik since Roman times, taking advantage of the great rock outcrop for protection. In the 14th century, Bulgar Tsar Ivan Stratsimir developed the site. After the Ottomans conquered the castle in 1396, they expanded it further, using it as a base.

OPPOSITE AND ABOVE:

Carcassonne, Occitanie, France

The citadel within the town of Carcassonne has the largest intact wall of any town in Europe. It is protected by a double wall, the inner circuit dating to the Visigoths in the 7th century, the outer added after 1226, when Carcassonne passed to the French crown.

By the 19th century, the walls of Carcassonne were so derelict that the government ordered their demolition. Following public outcry, however, it was decided to restore the fortifications; the task was given to the architect and antiquarian Eugène Viollet-le-Duc in 1853. His creative reconstruction, however, was strongly criticized by some as being unsuitable for the climate and not in keeping with the broader architecture of the region.

OPPOSITE:

Castillo de Bellver, Spain
James II of Aragón and
Majorca constructed
Castillo de Bellver on the
Mediterranean island
of Majorca in the 14th
century. It is one of the
few circular castles in
Europe. The castle is well
preserved, thanks to the
fact that it was used as
a prison from the 18th
century until the middle
of the 20th century.

RIGHT:

Bač Fortress, Serbia
Bač was founded by
King Charles Robert I of
Hungary and Croatia in
1338. Its main purpose
was defence against
Ottoman encroachments,
and the site was further
developed in the 15th and
16th centuries. It fell to
the Ottomans after the
Battle of Mohács in 1526.

LEFT:
Bodiam Castle, England
Sir Edward Dalyngrigge's East Sussex home was built out of fear of French raids, but the old-fashioned walls of Bodiam suggest greater interest in show than defence.

ABOVE:
Raby Castle, Darlington, England
The Neville family built Raby Castle in County Durham between 1367 and 1390. It passed to royal control in the 16th century after the Rising of the North, an unsuccessful attempt by Catholic nobles to depose Protestant Elizabeth I. The Vane family bought the castle along with Barnard Castle in 1626 and it remains the principal seat of the Barons Barnard.

ALL PHOTOGRAPHS:

Bran Castle, Romania

Known as 'Dracula's Castle', Bran was first constructed as a wooden fortress in 1212 to guard Bran Gorge. The stone castle now on the site was started in 1377, and soon saw service defending the Transylvania/Wallachia border against Ottoman attack. After the Ottoman threat receded, Bran Castle became a customs post.

Hungary ceded Bran Castle to Romania in 1920 in the Treaty of Trianon and it became a Romanian royal residence. The communist government expelled Romania's royal family in 1948. In 2009, after a legal battle, ownership was officially transferred to the American Archduke Dominic von Habsburg.

Koluvere Castle, Western Estonia

Constructed on an artificial island in the Liivi River, the high, square tower is the earliest part of Koluvere Castle, constructed in the early 13th century. The round tower was added in the 16th century, its shape providing a more stable firing platform and better defence against cannon.

Beersel Castle, Belgium

Erected between 1300 and 1310 to protect Brussels, Beersel's wide moat compensates for its lack of elevation. Beersel suffered sieges in the 14th and 15th centuries, but each time the damage was soon repaired. The castle housed a cotton factory for nearly a century before its restoration as a tourist site.

Khotyn Fortress, Chernivtsi Oblast, Ukraine

Khotyn stands on the right bank of the Dniester River and a fortress has guarded the area since the 10th century. The first fortress was a simple artificial mound with a stockade on top. The current castle was begun in 1325, with major additions in the 1380s and 1460s. Khotyn owes its massive wall – 5–6m (16–20ft) wide and up to 40m (130ft) high – to Stephen the Great of Moldavia (1457–1504). The expense was soon justified, as Khotyn successfully resisted a siege by the Ottoman sultan Mehmed II in 1476.

Srebrenik Fortress, Bosnia

First mentioned in 1333, Srebrenik Fortress occupies a
high, inaccessible rock. The ruins mostly date to the 14th
century, although the Ottomans made improvements,
including a mosque. The site was probably abandoned in
the 16th century. Modern visitors reach the castle via a
footbridge from a neighbouring hill.

ABOVE:

Karlštejn Castle, Czech Republic

Holy Roman Emperor Charles IV had this castle erected
between 1348 and 1365; for decades its treasury housed
the imperial regalia. During the Hussite siege of 1422,
the defenders succumbed to disease after the attackers
catapulted corpses and 2,000 cartloads of manure over
the walls.

Oberhofen Castle, Switzerland

After occupying a fort in the hills above Oberhofen, the von Eschenbach family moved to the shore of Lake Thun and began constructing the current castle in around 1200. The gatehouse still attests to the castle's originally strong fortification, which included a moat on the landward side. In 1306, the Habsburgs forced the von Eschenbach family to sell Oberhofen Castle to them. But after the Swiss Federation decisively defeated the Habsburgs at the Battle of Sempach (1386), the canton of Bern took control of the castle, before selling it to one of the leading families of the city.

BOTH PHOTOGRAPHS:

Sea Castle, Sidon, Lebanon

Crusaders constructed Sea Castle on an island off the Mediterranean coast in 1228. The castle was partly destroyed by the Mamluks, but they later rebuilt it, adding the 50m (150ft) long causeway connecting it to the mainland. Sea Castle was still a viable fortress as late as 1840, when the British navy bombarded the stronghold, part of Britain's intervention in the Egyptian–Ottoman War (1839–1842). The cannonballs still embedded in the sea wall *(above)* attest to the strength of the fortress's construction.

ALL PHOTOGRAPHS:

Citadel of Qaitbay, Egypt
Mamluk sultan al-Ashraf
Qaitbay established this
citadel in 1477 to protect
Alexandria's harbour
from the growing threat
of the Ottoman fleet. It
stands on the exact site
of the ancient Lighthouse
of Alexandria, part of
which was still standing
in the 15th century. Many
of the lighthouse's stones
were used to construct
the fort. A lover of fine
architecture, Sultan
al-Ashraf Qaitbay spent
100,000 dinars to make
his citadel beautiful. The
Ottomans continued to
maintain it after they
took Egypt in 1512.
Qaitbay's citadel was
badly damaged when
the British bombarded
Alexandria in 1882, but
was reconstructed in the
20th century.

ABOVE:

Gyantse Dzong, Tibet

Constructed in 1268, Gyantse Fortress guarded the
approach to the city of Lhasa. The castle suffered in
the 20th century when the British expedition to Tibet
(1903–04) attacked Gyantse and a lucky strike hit the
castle's powder magazine. Then, in 1967, the Chinese
dynamited the fortress. It was only gradually restored.

OPPOSITE:

Castle of Astypalaia, Greece

The Venetian patrician family of Querini controlled the
island of Astypalaia from 1207 to 1522. In 1413 they
developed the castle into its current form as a base against
frequent pirate attack. In a distinctive feature, the castle
walls lean at several points on reinforced house walls,
providing a second protective ring.

ALL PHOTOGRAPHS:

The Palace of the Grand Master of the Knights, Rhodes, Greece

Also known as the Kastello, the grand master's palace was the citadel and administrative centre of the Knights Hospitaller after they occupied the island of Rhodes in 1309. The Knights developed an existing Byzantine fortress, creating a rare masterpiece of Gothic architecture in the eastern Mediterranean.

ALL PHOTOGRAPHS:

**Coca Castle,
Segovia, Spain**

The archbishop of Seville began construction of this well-preserved castle in 1448; work continued until the end of the 15th century. Coca is constructed of brick because of lack of good building stone in the region. The castle never suffered a serious attack; its impressive defences may have been largely for show.

This is the best example of Mudéjar castle-building on the Iberian Peninsula. The Christian architect incorporated many elements of Islamic art, fusing the style into an overall late Gothic design. Primarily used as a residence, Coca Castle now houses a school.

LEFT:

Kasteel van Arenberg, Belgium

The medieval castle on this site was demolished and work started on the Kasteel van Arenberg in 1455. It was intended from the first as a palace rather than a fortress; although the Kasteel includes strong towers, its large windows would have made defence against attack impossible.

OPPOSITE:

Doorwerth Castle, Netherlands

After destruction of an earlier keep on the site, Doorwerth was rebuilt in the 14th century and enlarged in the 15th and 16th centuries. Doorwerth was damaged by Allied shelling in World War II, but has since been restored and now houses three museums.

ALL PHOTOGRAPHS:

Odescalchi Castle, Italy
Standing on the south shore of Lake Bracciano, Odescalchi Castle is only 29km (18 miles) from Rome. It probably started as a tower built in the 10th century to protect the area from Saracen attack, but the current structure was undertaken by Napoleone Orsini from 1470.

The Orsini owners of Odescalchi Castle were inveterate enemies of the Borgia pope Alexander VI (1492–1503), who on two separate occasions sent one of his sons with an army to besiege the castle. Odescalchi successfully resisted both sieges and remains a magnificent example of Renaissance military architecture.

Kamianets-Podilskyi Castle, Belarus

A vital defence on the Polish–Lithuanian frontier, the castle at Kamianets-Podilskyi was probably first erected in the early 13th century. It was modernized shortly after 1400 and again a century and a half later. The castle held out against assaults by Cossacks, Ottomans, and a staggering 51 attacks from the Mongols.

BELOW:

Golubac Fortress, Serbia

The castle near Golubac is strategically located on the south bank of the Danube, in border territory that has been contested repeatedly. It is not clear who built Golubac, but construction was probably in the 14th century. At various times Bulgarians, Hungarians, Turks, Serbs and Austrians have claimed the castle.

Donegal Castle, Ireland

The castle in Donegal originally consisted of a 15th-century rectangular keep, built as a stronghold for the O'Donnell clan. When the O'Donnell leaders fled Ireland in 1611, Donegal Castle was granted to an Englishman, who added a comfortable Jacobean wing. The castle was restored in the 1990s.

Oxburgh Hall, Norfolk, England

Sir Edmund Bedingfeld began construction of Oxburgh Hall in around 1482. It is still owned by his descendants, although now administered by the National Trust. Oxburgh is a moated country house. It looks imposing but would not have been able to hold out against determined assault.

Trakai Island, Lithuania
Grand Duke Kestutis began constructing Trakai on an island in Lake Galve in the 14th century. The castle was damaged in an attack by the Teutonic Knights in 1377, but during a truce the duke brought in the Order's own stonemason to rebuild the fortress. Sometimes called 'Little Marienburg', the castle is constructed of red brick in the style of Teutonic Order fortifications. A wooden footbridge now connects the castle to the mainland, but during its time as a Lithuanian royal centre the fortress would only have been accessible by boat.

ALL PHOTOGRAPHS:
Soroca Fort, Moldova
The castle in Soroca was built by order of Prince Stephen the Great of Moldavia, starting in 1499. It is one of a string of fortifications constructed along the Dnieper River to protect the Moldavian/Ukrainian frontier. Historians speculate that Prince Stephen of Moldavia brought in western European architects to design his castle. It was engineered in the late medieval western fashion, with curved walls and round outer towers, better able to resist cannon fire.

The castle was still of military importance during the campaigns of Peter the Great in the early 18th century.

OPPOSITE AND BELOW:

Cittadella, Island of Gozo, Malta

The medieval castle on Gozo was obsolete by the time the Ottomans invaded the Mediterranean island in 1551; they soon captured it, enslaving the 6,000 people who had taken refuge there. The south walls were rebuilt to repel gunpowder attacks in 1599–1622, but the medieval north walls were left intact.

ALL PHOTOGRAPHS:

Forchtenstein Castle, Austria

The earliest part of Forchtenstein is its 50m (160ft) high keep, constructed in the early 15th century. In the early 17th century, the site passed to Count Nicolas Esterházy, who brought in Italian architects to transform the castle into a sumptuous residence. The Esterházys still own Forchtenstein today.

ALL PHOTOGRAPHS:

Royal Fort, Lahore, Pakistan

The citadel on the north side of Lahore was fortified in the 11th century, but the Mughal emperor Akbar laid the foundations for the current edifice in 1566. The large, 20-hectare (50-acre) site was almost completely rebuilt in the 17th century by Akbar's successors, include Shah Jahan, who also commissioned the Taj Mahal.

Caernarfon Castle, Wales

Caernarfon Castle was an important part of King Edward I of England's plan to establish permanent control over Wales with a series of strong castles. Caernarfon was begun in 1283 as an administrative centre for northern Wales. Perhaps because of the great expense involved, the interior was never completed.

Caernarfon's strategic location on the coast of northern Wales made it a logical place for Edward I to construct a castle, but it fell into disrepair in the 16th century when English–Welsh tensions were lowered. Nonetheless, Caernarfon remained strong enough to withstand three Parliamentary sieges in the 1640s.

ABOVE:

Krujë Castle, Albania

Krujë Castle's origins are obscure, although the current structures are late medieval. Krujë is a famous centre of Albanian resistance. When local patriot Skanderbeg rebelled against Ottoman rule, he withstood massive sieges of Krujë in 1450, 1466 and 1467.

OPPOSITE:

Zilkale Castle, Turkey

The castle at Zilkale was probably constructed by the Byzantine ruler of Trebizond in the 13th century. From its position at the edge of a cliff, Zilkale overlooks an important trade route. When the Ottomans took the region in the 16th century, they continued to use the castle.

Herstmonceux Castle, East Sussex, England
When Henry VI's treasurer wanted a residence to reflect his social importance in 1441, he rebuilt the family's manor house on a grand scale. One of the oldest brick buildings in England, Herstmonceux Castle has some decorative elements of a castle, such as crenellations and towers, but it is a palace rather than a fortress.

Kilchurn Castle, Scotland

Now a picturesque ruin, most of Kilchurn Castle was constructed in the mid-15th century as a base for a cadet branch of the Campbell clan in the central Highlands. When the Campbells of Glenorchy became earls of Breadalbane, they abandoned Kilchurn, which was a ruin by around 1770.

The castle's earliest element was a five-storey keep, constructed around 1450. A wall around the whole small island created a protected courtyard for other buildings. At the time, the castle could only be reached by a causeway at low tide.

ALL PHOTOGRAPHS:

Fortifications of Kotor, Montenegro

Although there have been fortifications on this site since the Byzantine era, the extensive fortifications near the town of Kotor were began by the Venetians in the 14th century. The fortifications have had a colourful history. The Ottomans successfully besieged the city and occupied the area from 1538 to 1571. In 1797 it passed to the control of the Habsburg monarchy. In 1979 the walls were damaged by an earthquake, but today the city is listed as a UNESCO World Heritage Site.

Early Modern Period: 1500–1750

Many areas of the world still had an active need for fortifications during the early modern period – especially with the advent of gunpowder weapons – but increasingly aristocrats built castles for show and esteem rather than defence. The castles of this era provide a useful clue to how settled conditions were in various regions of the world. The Mediterranean, North Africa, the Near East, Eastern Europe and Latin America could all still expect attacks from nearby determined enemies, as the strength and design of the castles in these regions attest. By contrast, the British Isles had little to fear from organized armies, and the stately houses of England, Scotland, Wales and Ireland were built for comfort and status rather than protection and warfare. Many still incorporated elements of traditional castle architecture – such as towers, curtain walls, crenellations, and even moats – as symbols of authority and prestige. The same can be said of many castles in Japan and China during this period.

OPPOSITE:
Red Fort, Delhi, India
The Mughal emperor Shah Jahan began construction of the Red Fort in 1638 after he decided to move his capital from Agra to Delhi. Constructed of local red sandstone, the palace complex is enclosed by a 2.4km (1.5 mile) long wall and covers an area of more than 100 hectares (250 acres).

Mehrangarh Fort, Jodhpur, Rajasthan, India
Mehrangarh stands on a 125m (410ft) hill overlooking
the city of Jodhpur; Rao Jodha founded both the
city and the castle in around 1460, seeking greater
security in the frequent wars of the region. Most of the
fortress, though, dates from the mid-17th century, as its
elaborate palaces attest.

Osaka Castle, Japan
A castle was begun in
Osaka in 1583 but was
soon burned during the
wars to unite Japan. The
Tokugawa clan seized
the shogunate and began
construction of a new
castle in 1620, creating
an edifice that was highly
defensible but also a
monument to the family's
prestige and power.

Matsumoto Castle, Japan
All that remains of
Matsumoto Castle near
Tokyo is the keep, which
was constructed in the
later 16th century. It still
has its original stone
and woodwork and is
regarded as a national
treasure. Matsumoto
Castle originally also had
interconnecting walls,
moats and gatehouses.

Marmaris Castle, Turkey
Herodotus says that the first fortress at Marmaris was constructed in 3000 BCE. The castle as we see it today, however, is the work of Ottoman sultan Suleiman the Magnificent, who had Marmaris Castle erected in 1522 to support his attack against the island of Rhodes.

Egeskov Castle, Funen, Denmark

The best-preserved Renaissance water castle in Europe, construction of Egeskov began in 1554. Civil unrest at the time made defences desirable, so Egeskov was built on oak piles sunk into the centre of a small lake – the enormous number of trees needed gave the castle its name, which means 'oak forest'.

ALL PHOTOGRAPHS:

Château de Chambord, France

The largest of the Loire châteaux, Chambord was constructed between 1519 and 1547 as a hunting lodge for King Francis I. Although the château has a central keep, four great towers, and even a partial moat, these elements were anachronistic when they were built, and probably intended for decoration, not defence.

ALL PHOTOGRAPHS:

Red Fort, Delhi, India
The Red Fort was the chief residence of India's Mughal emperors from its completion in 1648 until 1857. Despite its strong defences, the last Mughal ruler, Bahadur Shah II, did not try to defend his palace in 1857 when the British attacked while suppressing the Indian Mutiny. British troops systematically plundered the Red Fort in 1857, destroying much of the marble work besides carrying off or wrecking furniture and more portable wealth. However, enough remains to appreciate the unique style of decoration that Shah Jahan favoured, a pleasing mixture of Persian, European, and Indian artistic elements.

Nakhal Fort, Oman

Nakhal Fort began as a Sassanian defence against Arabic raiders, perhaps in the 6th century. It was reconstructed in the 17th century because of an ongoing need to protect the oasis and trade route at the base of Mt Nakhal. The fort is in pristine shape today thanks to a 1990 renovation.

Nakhal was still a working fortress through much of the 19th century. The current gateway and outer walls were added in 1834 by Imam Said bin Sultan. The lower fortress contains a mosque and a facility to store the dates harvested from the palm trees that surround the fort. The fortress has a completely irregular plan, since the castle was built onto a natural rock outcrop; at points within the fort the rock juts up into the living and working space.

Kyrenia Castle, Cyprus

Cyprus has been fought over for centuries, and the Venetian conquest (1489) reduced the port of Kyrenia's castle to ruins. The Venetian authorities reconstructed the castle in 1540, designing thicker walls, cannon embrasures and ramps to deploy cannon.

Fasil Ghebbi, Ethiopia

Emperor Fasilides (1632–67) was the first ruler of Ethiopia to establish a permanent capital, and Fasil Ghebbi was constructed as his residence. Fasilides and his successors built palaces within the enclosure that he created by means of a curtain wall, pierced by 12 gates.

LEFT:

Fort Metal Cross, Ghana

Originally naming it Dixcove Fort, the British began construction of Fort Metal Cross in 1692. Their purpose was trade for gold with inland regions, which put them in competition with Dutch traders. Local chiefs shifted their support between the Europeans, several times besieging Fort Metal Cross on behalf of the Dutch.

ABOVE:

Cape Coast Castle, Ghana

One of the infamous 'slave castles' of the Gold Coast, the Swedish African Company first constructed Cape Coast Castle in 1650. The castle changed hands many times, most owners seeking profit from the transatlantic slave trade. The castle's dungeons could hold up to 1,000 captives, awaiting shipment to the Americas.

ALL PHOTOGRAPHS:

Krzyztopór Castle, Poland

Krzyztopór had a very short history as a viable fortress. It was probably completed in 1644. Swedish forces, however, occupied the castle in the invasion of 1655–1657, causing so much damage that the decision was made not to rebuild it. Destruction was completed by Russian troops in 1770.

For about a century after the castle was damaged by the Swedes, several Polish noble families continued to live in the best-preserved part of the castle. Today, about 90 per cent of the castle's external walls still stand, but the buildings within Krzyztopór are in a ruinous state.

Santa Rosa Castle, Venezuela

Constructed in 1677–1683 after the town of La Asunsión suffered an attack from French pirates, for centuries this colonial fortress has protected access to La Asunsión. Santa Rosa continued to have a military function until 1935, after which it became a war museum.

Castillo San Felipe de Barajas, Colombia

Latin America's most impressive defensive complex, the castle of San Felipe was begun in 1536 and expanded in 1657 to protect the port of Cartagena by land and sea. Its walls form a complex pattern of bunkers; they and the bastions reinforce each other. Expansive subterranean tunnels aid internal communications.

OPPOSITE:

Parke's Castle, Ireland

Sir Roger Parke was granted the O'Rourke estate on the bank of Loch Gill in the 1610s. Parke constructed a fortified manor house in place of the earlier castle, combining defensive elements with comfort. Although not strong enough to withstand an army, Parke's Castle provided protection from local peasants.

RIGHT:

Drumlanrig Castle, Scotland

This Dumfriesshire stately home, which includes 120 rooms, was constructed between 1679 and 1689 of the local pink sandstone; it is a fine example of late Renaissance architecture.

ABOVE:

Maruševec Castle, Croatia

This fine Croatian castle was constructed in 1547 and
enlarged in 1618. In style it is a mostly Renaissance
edifice, although small neo-Gothic towers were added in
the 19th century. Nationalized by Croatia's communist
government in 1945, in the early 2000s Maruševec was
returned to the Pongratz family.

OPPOSITE:

Trolle-Ljungby Castle, Sweden

A castle on the site of Trolle-Ljungby underwent
major reconstruction starting in 1621, creating today's
Renaissance-style manor house. Originally owned by
Danish nobles, it was attacked during the Swedish
conquest of the province of Scania in the 1650s; bullet
holes can still be seen on its walls.

Nesvizh Castle, Belarus

Although it was built on medieval foundations, Nesvizh Castle was constructed in 1582–1604 as a Renaissance palace. A Swedish army under Charles XII sacked the castle and destroyed its fortifications in 1706. It was then renovated in Baroque style. During the Soviet period, Nesvizh was used as a sanatorium.

ALL PHOTOGRAPHS:

Changdeok Palace, South Korea

The Joseon Dynasty originally built 'Prospering Virtue Palace' in 1392 as one of its five great palaces, but the original building was destroyed in the Japanese invasion of 1592 and rebuilt in 1610. The palace complex consists of 13 buildings, enclosed within a stout wall in the heart of Seoul. The lovely detail work (*below*) of Changdeok Palace attests to its role as the principal residence of the rulers of Korea for 270 years, from the time of its rebuilding in 1610 until almost 1900. The palace's extensive gardens help create a harmonious atmosphere.

Kasbah Ras el-Ain, Morocco
The Moroccan ruler Moulay Ismail developed the town of Beni Mellal in 1688 and constructed Ras el-Ain to protect a spring on the cliff above the town. Constructed of stone and rammed earth (*pisé*), Ras el-Ain is in excellent condition and dominates the surrounding countryside.

ALL PHOTOGRAPHS:

Fortifications of Mdina, Malta

The small town of Mdina in northern Malta has been fortified since at least the 11th century. The defences were improved by the Knights Hospitallers after they occupied the Mediterranean island in 1530 and again in the mid-17th century. The walls were rebuilt yet again in 1722, incorporating Baroque elements.

173

ALL PHOTOGRAPHS:
Gripsholm Castle, Sweden

A Carthusian monastery stood on the site of Gripsholm Castle until 1526, when the newly Protestant king ordered its destruction. In its place, Gustav Vasa ordered the construction of a royal castle.

The castle overlooking Lake Mälaren was renovated as a favoured royal residence in 1773, the new work including a theatre in one of the towers. It underwent a controversial restoration in the period 1889–94, with the architect Fredrik Liljekvist removing many of the alterations from the 17th and 18th centuries.

LEFT:

Inveraray Castle, Scotland

Work on Inveraray Castle began in 1746, the new edifice replacing a 15th-century castle. Inveraray is one of the earliest examples of Gothic Revival architecture; the conical roofs on the corner towers were added after a fire in 1877.

OPPOSITE:

Belvoir Castle, Leicestershire, England

The seat of the Dukes of Rutland, Belvoir was constructed between 1654 and 1668 after the former castle was destroyed during the Civil War. Belvoir was then renovated in the Gothic Revival style. It was almost completely destroyed by fire in 1816, but was reconstructed following the same plan.

Castillo de San Pedro de la Roca, Cuba

This fortress on the coast near the city of Santiago de Cuba was constructed between 1638 and 1700; a series of fortified terraces was designed to fit the castle on the steep promontory. The fortress was partially destroyed by English privateers in 1662 before it was completed; but when finished the Castillo successfully beat off several English and French attacks.

ALL PHOTOGRAPHS:
Bojnice Castle, Slovakia
Although first mentioned in a document of 1013, Bojnice Castle bears little resemblance to the small wooden fortress of the 11th century. The castle was gradually rebuilt in stone, and in the 16th century was transformed into a Renaissance castle.

Bojnice is now a 19th-century romantic fairy-tale castle, thanks to the rebuilding masterminded by its owner Count János Ferenc Pálffy between 1888 and 1910. Deeply impressed by the French châteaux of the Loire Valley, Pálffy invested a fortune in recreating this French style in Slovakia.

Modern Era: 1750–Present

For most people in the modern world, the very word 'castle' evokes a romantic, fairy-tale structure inhabited by aristocratic knights and noble ladies. A number of men and women in the 19th and 20th centuries – whether they should be regarded as rich eccentrics, visionaries or opportunists – recreated an idealized, medieval past by building castles and castle-like structures of their own. Such edifices do indeed evoke fairy tales and the atmosphere of an imagined past, and it is hardly surprising that a number of recent romantic movies were filmed in modern rather than medieval castles. Even in the 20th century, however, castles in some regions continued to be constructed for military purposes. Some, in places such as the United Arab Emirates, are still sites of romantic appeal. It is important to remember, though, that the functional steel and concrete bunkers of the Channel Islands or the starkness of a Maunsell Fort from World War II are heirs to both the name and function of castles.

OPPOSITE:
Castillo de Butrón, Spain
Butrón Castle was the hobby of the wealthy Marqués Francisco de Cubas, who from 1878 almost entirely rebuilt the medieval castle. Resting on cement foundations, the towers are modelled on those of 19th-century Bavarian castles. Visually stunning, Butrón was very inconvenient to live in and soon fell out of use.

ALL PHOTOGRAPHS:
**Hwaseong Fortress,
Suwon, South Korea**
King Jeongjo constructed
Hwaseong Fortress from
1794 to 1796 to honour
the remains of his father,
but the work also reflects
Jeongjo's desire to move
his capital from Seoul to
Suwon, 30km (19 miles)
to the south. Hwaseong's
5.7km (3.5 mile) wall
surrounds most of the city
centre; the whole complex
took 700,000 man-hours
to build.

Bithnah Fort, United Arab Emirates
This strong fortress, strategically located on Wadi Ham, helped assure the independence of the emirate of Fujairah. It was probably constructed in the early 19th century to protect the area from Wahhabi attacks, but may date as early as the aftermath of the Battle of Bithnah in 1745.

ABOVE:
Le Mirage, Namib Desert, Namibia
A luxury resort and spa located in the Namib Desert, Le Mirage has the appearance of a rather dilapidated North African fortress on the outside; but the spacious courtyard has been designed as a lush oasis, complete with a large swimming pool.

FOLLOWING PAGES:
Al Jahili Fort, United Arab Emirates
Sheikh Zayed I constructed Al Jahili in the 1890s as a summer residence, but it also protected the palm farmers of Al Jahili oasis and kept peace among the local Bedouin. Each side of the square mud-brick fortress measures 35m (115ft); the walls stand 8m (26ft) high.

Peckforton Castle, England

Peckforton was constructed in 1844–50 as a Gothic Revival recreation of a late medieval castle. Besides the usual towers, architect Anthony Salvin included a portcullis and dry moat, and even went so far as to design exterior windows that are little more than arrow slits. Wealthy Cheshire landowner and MP John Tollemache spent the enormous sum of £60,000 on constructing Peckforton, even having a railway laid to transport building stone from the quarry a mile away. The American Evelyn Graybill purchased Peckforton in 1988 and turned the castle into a hotel.

Hluboká nad Vltavou Castle, Czech Republic
Long owned by the wealthy Schwarzenberg family,
Hluboká Castle has been transformed many times over
the centuries. The castle was first built in the second
half of the 13th century, but was rebuilt in Renaissance,
Baroque and, in 1841–71, Gothic Revival style.

Hluboká nad Vltavou Castle, Czech Republic

Hluboká Castle owes its current form to Johann Adolf II von Schwarzenberg, who had it remodelled in the style of Windsor Castle. He also designed a large English garden around the castle. The last Schwarzenberg owner of Hluboká was an outspoken critic of the Nazis and fled when the Germans invaded Czechoslovakia; the occupying Germans seized Hluboká. After World War II, the Czech government confiscated Hluboká by special legislative act and it remains state-owned.

ABOVE:

Dunrobin Castle, Scotland

The second Duke of Sutherland commissioned architect Sir Charles Barry to rebuild Dunrobin Castle in the fashionable Gothic style between 1835 and 1850. With 189 rooms, this is the largest stately home in the northern Highlands. Much of the interior had to be rebuilt after a fire in 1915.

RIGHT:

Vajdahunyad Castle, Hungary

Originally built in cardboard and wood in Budapest's city park for the Millennial Exhibition of 1896, Vajdahunyad was so popular that it was rebuilt in stone in 1904–8. The castle includes elements of great Hungarian buildings, so parts of the building are in Romanesque, Gothic, Renaissance and Baroque styles.

ALL PHOTOGRAPHS:

Pena Palace, Portugal

A monastery once stood on this site in the Sintra Mountains, but it was destroyed in the Great Lisbon Earthquake of 1755. King Ferdinand acquired the ruin in 1837 and commissioned a mining engineer and amateur architect, Wilhelm Ludwig von Eschwege, to create a romantic castle.

Constructed between 1842 and 1854, Pena is an eclectic but surprisingly harmonious building. It is for the most part a neo-Gothic structure, but also includes Islamic architectural and decorative elements. Following the Republican Revolution of 1910, Pena Palace became a national property.

ALL PHOTOGRAPHS:

Hohenzollern Castle, Germany

A castle has stood on this site in southwest Germany since the early 11th century; it gave the Hohenzollern family its name. The current castle was constructed in 1846–67 by order of King Friedrich Wilhelm IV of Prussia. It is mostly in Gothic Revival style but also includes elements of French château architecture. A monument to the German romantic movement, the third and last Hohenzollern Castle was intended as a showplace; the royal family of Prussia never regularly occupied it. The Hohenzollern family still own the castle; the Prussian flag flies above it when a family member is in residence.

Neuschwanstein Castle, Germany

Despite hordes of tourists (about 1.3 million each year), Neuschwanstein is a magical place that dominates the countryside from its perch in the Alpine foothills in southern Bavaria. It was the creation of King Ludwig II of Bavaria (reigned 1864–86), whose extravagance led to him being declared insane and deposed. Begun in 1869, the castle wasn't completed when Ludwig died in 1886. The castle's enormous Throne Hall (*opposite right*) was designed to emulate the Grail Hall of Wagner's opera *Parzifal*, the king's favourite composer. The style is eclectic, including Romanesque, Gothic and Byzantine elements.

ALL PHOTOGRAPHS:

Lichtenstein Castle, Germany

Count Wilhelm von Urach was a dedicated medievalist and was inspired by Wilhelm Hauff's 1826 novel *Lichtenstein* to create a medieval castle as his home in southwest Germany. The result, completed in 1842, was Lichtenstein Castle. After the 1848 revolution, Lichtenstein was made defensible with outworks and a trench, and cannon mounted on the walls.

Mamula Island, Montenegro

An Austrian admiral designed the fortress that covers 90 per cent of Mamula Island in 1853. Just off the Adriatic coast, it guards the entrance to Boka Kotorska Bay. With its squat, bunker-like construction and thick walls, Mamula Fort is a good example of defensive architecture in the age of heavy cannon. By the early 20th century, Mamula Fort was being used as a prison for sailors; in 1942, the Italian government made it a concentration camp. Mamula was infamous for torture and cruelty to prisoners. Despite survivors' protests, a plan was announced in 2016 to transform the fortress into a luxury hotel.

ALL PHOTOGRAPHS:

Telouet Kasbah, Telouet, Morocco

The mud-brick Telouet Kasbah (citadel) is gradually crumbling, but still exists as a monument to the power of the El Glaoui family. It was constructed in the 1860s in the High Atlas to control the caravan route from the Sahara to Marrakesh.

Telouet Kasbah consists of a maze of rooms, the reception halls of the El Glaoui pashas still existing in surprisingly good condition.

The El Glaoui were virtually independent rulers of the region; they constructed Telouet Kasbah beside the ruins of an earlier fortress to demonstrate their power and wealth.

ALL PHOTOGRAPHS:

Castle Muromtsevo, Russia

Count Vladimir Khrapovitsky visited France in 1880 and returned home determined to build himself a medieval castle. He realized his dream in the period 1884–89, creating Russia's only Gothic castle. The magnificent 80-room structure housed a forestry technical school after the Russian Revolution of 1917, but now lies abandoned.

ALL PHOTOGRAPHS:
Bory Castle, Hungary
Planned by architect and sculptor Jenö Bory (1879–1959), this modern castle was almost completely the work of one man. For nearly 40 summers, when he did not have academic duties, Bory constructed his castle with only one or two assistants and decorated it with his sculptures.

A unique castle constructed entirely from concrete, Bory Castle is a monument to Jenö Bory's love for his wife, the artist Ilona Komocsin, whose paintings also adorn the interior. The family still lives there, but recently established a foundation to help pay for the upkeep of the large castle and grounds.

ALL PHOTOGRAPHS:

De Haar Castle, Utrecht, Netherlands

A monument to the wealth of the Rothschild family, De Haar was almost entirely rebuilt in 1892–1902 in the neo-Gothic style by Dutch architect Pierre Cuypers for Baroness Hélène de Rothschild. The 200-bedroom palace had all the latest luxuries, including steam-operated central heating. The oldest record of De Haar Castle dates from 1391. Mostly torn down in the late 15th century, it was rebuilt in the 16th, only to decline into a ruinous state. The c. 1900 reconstruction preserved the existing lower walls, but little else.

213

Hatley Castle, Victoria, Canada

In 1906, Lieutenant-Governor James Dunsmuir of British Columbia and his wife commissioned this 40-room mansion. It is largely constructed of concrete and was designed in the Tudor revival style popular in the Edwardian era. The massive Edwardian garden enhances the castle's effect. Hatley Castle was sold after its original owners died.

In 1940, the Canadian government purchased it and used it as a training establishment for the navy. Hatley now houses Royal Roads University.

ALL PHOTOGRAPHS:

Hearst Castle, USA
Newspaper magnate William Randolph Hearst first asked architect Julia Morgan to design a 'bungalow' on his family ranch in California. Plans rapidly grew; today the Casa Grande *(opposite)* at the centre of the castle complex has an area of 20,880 square metres (68,500 sq ft). It is modelled on a Spanish church, not a castle.

A feature of the castle is that ceilings and whole façades from historic European buildings were incorporated into the mansion as it was built. The Neptune Pool includes the façade of an ancient Roman temple, while a number of vaulted ceilings were originally made for Spanish monasteries *(left)*.

OPPOSITE:
Swallow's Nest Palace, Ukraine
This bijou neo-Gothic castle was designed with only three bedrooms. It was constructed in 1911–12 for the Baltic German businessman Baron von Steingel. Perched on a 40m (130ft) high cliff overlooking the Black Sea, Swallow's Nest is often invoked as a symbol of Ukraine. It is now a restaurant.

RIGHT:
Wadi Dhar Rock Palace, Yemen
Growing out of the rock on which it perches, Wadi Dhar was constructed in the 1920s for Imam Yahya Muhammad Hamidlin, the ruler of Yemen, as a summer retreat. It largely replaced a structure dating from 1786.

Red Sands, Maunsell Forts, Thames Estuary, England

Guy Maunsell designed armed towers to protect the English coast in World War II. Red Sands is of the type manned by the army; it consists of seven interconnected steel platforms, designed to spot and then to bring down enemy aircraft.

World War II forts, Guernsey

The German fortifications of Guernsey are a monument to Hitler's obsession with holding some British soil. Although the island had no military significance, during the German occupation of 1940–45 they created a massive defence programme.

LEFT:

Moussa Castle, Lebanon

Moussa Abdel Karim al-Maamari loved the Middle Ages and as a boy dreamed of building a castle. He single-mindedly pursued his goal, gaining experience with restoration work, then starting Moussa Castle in 1962, which took him 50 years to complete.

RIGHT:

Ravadinovo Castle, Bulgaria

Ravadinovo, nicknamed 'The Castle in Love with the Wind', is extraordinary. Architect Georgi Kostadinov Tumpalov began construction in 1996. The huge cross-shaped edifice is made of marble limestone, full of micro diamonds that change colour in the light.

Picture Credits